NEXT PRACTICES

Being Better
Than Best in
Online Recruitment

Short Takes
for Time Challenged Pros
Who Want to Perform
at Their Peak

Most WEDDLE's books are available at Amazon.com and in bulk quantities through Independent Publishers Group, 814 North Franklin Street, Chicago, IL 60610, ph: 312-337-0747, www.ipgbook.com. For other titles, please visit Weddles.com or contact WEDDLE's at 203-964-1888.

ISBN: 978-1-928734-83-3

WEDDLE's
www.weddles.com
2052 Shippan Avenue
Stamford, CT 06902

Where People Matter Most.

Praise for Peter Weddle's Books and Guides

WEDDLE's Guide to Employment Sites on the Internet

"Restaurant patrons looking for quality dining have Zagat to guide their cuisine needs. For the recruitment industry, the name is Weddle … Peter Weddle that is."

American Staffing Association

"I've known Peter Weddle for years. He is an immensely likeable guy. He is also extremely knowledgeable. Highly recommended!"

Richard Nelson Bolles, What Color is Your Parachute?

"A wealth of updated and useful information."

Library Journal

"WEDDLE's is a very useful tool that recruiters and HR professionals will find helpful."

Fortune Magazine

"When in doubt, consider WEDDLE's … an industry standard."

HR WIRE

"If you're looking for an objective guide to employment Web-sites, ExecuNet recommends WEDDLE's Guide."

ExecuNet Center for Executive Careers

Work Strong: Your Personal Career Fitness System

"Peter Weddle's Career Fitness System empowers you to take your job search to the next level and achieve lasting career success."

Diana Miller, CEO Community Job Club

"There are few people in the world who are as passionate about our careers and our own unique talents as Peter Weddle. *Work Strong* changes the paradigms of career management books and is sure to give you a new perspective on how to Work Strong in your own career."

Aaron Matos, CEO Jobing

"This book is a guide to finding yourself and to charting a new course for a 21st Century career. A must read!"

Kevin Wheeler, CEO Global Learning Resources, Inc.

"A lifetime of career happiness in a single book!"

Dan Honig, COO DiversityJobs.com

In today's world, it's not enough to work hard. You also have to work strong and perform at your peak. That's the power and promise of this book."

John Bell, CEO Boxwood Technology

Generalship: HR Leadership in a Time of War

"… a wake-up call for those of us in HR. We need to take on the accountability for effecting change. … This book provides a great strategy for doing just that."

Regina DeTore, VP/HR Sepracor, Inc.

"… a must-read book for human resource professionals, especially those who seek to be true leaders in their corporation."

Jerome N. Carter, SVP/HR International Paper

"Human Resources is now facing extra-ordinary challenges. This demanding time requires the kind of bold, thoughtful and thorough leadership suggested by this book."

Guy Patton, EVP/HR Fidelity Investments

"Don't miss this book. It's Machiavelli's *The Prince* and Covey's *7 Habits of Highly Effective People* all rolled into one for the HR profession."

Donna Introcaso, VP/HR iVillage

Recognizing Richard Rabbit: A Fable About Being True to Yourself

"A magical way to explore the essence of you."

Jennifer Floren, CEO Experience

"… a very intriguing and unique book."

Patrick Erwin, The Work Buzz CareerBuilder.com

"… if you're thinking about making changes in your personal life or want a pep talk about being true to yourself, check out this book."

Celeste Blackburn, Managing Editor Resources for Humans

"The story inspires useful reflection and a practical rethinking of your own personal effectiveness in work and life."

Jonathan Goodman, Review on Social Median

Career Fitness: How to Find, Win & Keep the Job You Want in the 1990s

"This book is phenomenal! It'll help you run the race of your life at work each day."

Harvey McKay, Swim With the Sharks Without Being Eaten Alive

"… street-smart wisdom, coupled with practical career workout tools … sure to be useful to people at any point in their career."

Madelyn Jennings, SVP/HR Gannett Company, Inc.

Also By Peter Weddle

A Multitude of Hope: A Novel About Rediscovering the American Dream

The Success Matrix: Wisdom from the Web on How to Get Hired & Not Be Fired

Job Nation: The 100 Best Employment Sites on the Web

The Career Activist Republic

Work Strong: Your Personal Career Fitness System

Recognizing Richard Rabbit: A Fable About Being True to Yourself

Generalship: HR Leadership in a Time of War

Career Fitness: How to Find, Win & Keep the Job You Want in the 1990s

Postcards from Space: Being the Best in Online Recruitment & HR Management

WEDDLE's Guide to Employment Sites on the Internet (biannually: 1999-present)

WEDDLE's Guide to Association Web Sites

WEDDLE'S Guide to Staffing Firms & Employment Agencies

'Tis of Thee: A Son's Search for the Meaning of Patriotism

Table of Contents

INTRODUCTION
WHAT'S NEXT?

I've written a biweekly newsletter about the art and science of online recruiting since 1999. By my calculation, that stretches across almost 400 issues and countless advances in technology, strategy and tactics. I started three years before Mark Zuckerberg matriculated at Harvard and met the roommates who would help him found Facebook, seven years before Twitter was launched and taught us to communicate in 140 characters or less and eleven years before Pinterest got its start and showed us how to crowdsource good ideas and products.

The newsletter began as a way to expand the readership of a biweekly column I was writing for the interactive edition of *The Wall Street Journal*. It soon took on a life of its own, however, as more and more recruiters wrote or called me about the challenges they were facing in the shifting dynamics of the War for Talent.

As I explored the impact of those changes and their implications for talent acquisition, it became clear to me that many of the so-called Best Practices in online recruiting were actually outmoded ideas. They were designed to fight the last war, rather than the current one. They were strategies and tactics to win the War for Any Talent – the shortfall in workers that existed in the late 20th and early 21st century – not the war in which we are presently engaged – the War for the Best Talent. And, today's war is a qualitative rather than a quantitative challenge; it is a quest for those scarce high performers who are essential to organizational success in a fiercely competitive global marketplace.

That realization led to the development of this book. It reprises and updates some of my most popular columns that deal, not with those Best Practices, but with **Next Practices** – the strategies and tactics for successful sourcing and recruiting in today's and tomorrow's War for the Best Talent. Each column is short and self-contained so the book can be comfortably read in the short intervals between requisitions, hiring manager conferences, prescreening calls, interviews and all the other responsibilities of a busy recruiter. They are, I believe, the way to be better than best in online recruiting.

Peter Weddle

Stamford, CT

NEXT PRACTICES
IN JOB POSTING

D espite the popularity of social recruiting these days, job postings remain the lingua franca of online recruitment. Whether they appear on a corporate career site, a job board or yes – on a social media site – job postings are the principal way most employers communicate their openings to top talent. Yet, most job postings still have the look and feel of old fashioned print classifieds. They are about as appealing as a statistics textbook written in Swahili.

How can you ensure your job postings communicate effectively with top talent?

IMPLEMENT THE FOLLOWING NEXT PRACTICES:
Don't Post a Job, Advertise Respect
Job Postings That Seduce Top Talent
A Social Job Posting
Application Triggers for Passive Prospects
Take Your Best Shot First

Don't Post a Job, Advertise Respect

Job postings are now routinely used on both job boards and social media sites. These online communications remain the most widespread method of candidate sourcing, yet are disparaged or simply ignored at almost every recruitment conference. Why? Because recruiters intuitively grasp the cost-benefit advantage of job postings, but all too often don't grab hold of their power. They use job postings to describe a job, when they would be better served by delivering respect.

There's been much written and spoken over the past couple of years about the importance of optimizing the candidate experience. In a highly competitive recruiting market, top performers will always gravitate to where they are treated best. As a consequence, the organization that gives candidates a distinctive and memorable experience will have a formidable advantage in the War for the Best Talent.

Such an experience is typically defined as what happens to a candidate while they are passing through an organization's recruiting process. For the candidate, however, the experience starts well before that point. It begins when they first encounter an employment opportunity. That interaction sets the tone for everything else that happens between the organization and the candidate.

Thanks to their heritage in print publications, job postings have traditionally been viewed as advertisements or announcements. Indeed, all too often, job postings are simply classified ad copy or position descriptions repurposed online. They seek to sell or inform, but not to engage the candidate. They generate applications from active job seekers, but have little or no impact on the passive prospects who make up the majority of the workforce.

What's the best way for your organization to engage that passive population? Publish job postings that shower the reader with respect. Use word choice and content to signal to the best of candidates that you recognize and value their talent.

A Respectful Job Posting

There are many facets to a "respectful job posting," but the following four are among the most important.

Number 1

Use vocabulary that corresponds to the reader's self image.

Top performers never think of themselves as a job seeker – a supplicant for work – even when they are in transition. Equally as important, they seldom have an up-to-date resume, so engage them by using more terms and phrases that are more relevant to them and thus more respectful. Address them as a "candidate" or "applicant" rather than as a "job seeker" and ask them to submit "an application" rather than "a resume."

Number 2

Tell the reader how long it will take to complete the application.

Top performers are almost always employed and, as a result, consider their time to be very valuable, so engage them by acknowledging and showing your respect for that point of view. Indicate how much time they will have to invest to complete the application for your opening and whether they must do so in a single sitting.

Number 3

Give the reader the information that's important to them.

Top performers don't care about an opening's requirements and responsibilities, so engage them by respecting their wishes and telling them what they do want to know: how your opening will enable them to continue as a top performer. Describe what they will get to do, learn and accomplish in your organization and the position and with whom they will get to work and how they will be recognized for their contribution.

Number 4

Show the reader that your organization is candidate-friendly.

Top performers don't like being left in the dark or ignored when they apply for an opening, so engage them by treating them as courteously as you would a guest. Explicitly state how long it normally takes for your organization to review an application and (if it's the case) that it will acknowledge the receipt of their application by email. Also provide the email address from which that message will arrive so they can ensure it doesn't get caught in their spam filter.

A job posting works best when it operates as a talent engagement platform rather than as an advertisement or announcement. And, engagement is best achieved with a posting that uses both vocabulary and content to convey an organization's respect for the reader.

Job Postings That Seduce Top Talent

There are just five rules for writing a job posting that will seduce even the most passive high caliber candidates. They are the key to successful recruitment advertising, whether you're posting your openings on a job board or a social media site, on a large and globally recognized site or a smaller, niche site with a particular specialization.

Why are these rules so important? Because passive, high caliber candidates are different from everyone else in the workforce. They are almost always employed. In order to recruit them, therefore, you have to persuade them to do the one thing we humans most hate to do: *change*. Your ad has to convince them to go from the devil they know – their current employer, boss and commute – to the devil they don't know – a new employer, a different boss and an unfamiliar commute.

Rule #1

Turn Titles into Magnets

Job postings are not help wanted announcements; they are electronic sales brochures. Their purpose is to sell top candidates on the opportunity inherent in an opening. That can't happen, however, unless those individuals are attracted to an opening and intrigued enough to pause and read it. So, give your job posting titles a magnetic pull by using the three most important triggers to action among passive prospects, separating each with a dash:

Location	Top talent want to work where they live so begin the title with the postal code abbreviation (e.g., CT) for the state or the name of the city in which the opening is located.
Skill	Top talent want to see themselves in the job, not pigeonholed into some HR job title (e.g., Programmer III) so indicate the skill (e.g., C++ Programmer) they use to describe the work they do.
Sizzle	Top talent are herd animals so ask the top performers in your organization why they came to work there and use that factor as the concluding element in your title. In other words, the final bit of information they receive should be what is most likely to differentiate your organization from other employers.

Here's how a good title might look for a programming position with a small but highly regarded company in Stamford, CT:

CT – C++ Programmer – Great team doing cutting edge work

Rule #2
Develop Content for Them, Not You

Requirements and responsibilities are words only employers could love. Top talent evaluate employment opportunities from an entirely different perspective. They want to know "what's in it for them" – how will a particular job advance them in their profession, craft or trade. So, describe your opening by answering five questions:

1	What will they get to do?
2	What will they get to learn?
3	What will they get to accomplish?
4	With whom will they get to work?
5	How will they be recognized and rewarded?

Rule #3
Sell First, Explain Later

Passive candidates have the attention span of a gnat, so it's critical that you lead with your strength when composing your ad. In effect, you have to convince them to read on before you can convince them your opening is right for them. So, begin every job posting with an enticement – a hard-hitting one-paragraph summary of why the position is a rare and extraordinary opportunity. First, tell them why it's a dream job with a dream employer and then provide the details of "what's in it for them."

Rule #4
Use a Format That Gnats Would Like

Given the short attention span of passive candidates, you have to make your message accessible in the blink of an eye. These individuals aren't in transition so they simply do not have the patience to plow through the thick, pithy paragraphs of a typical job posting. The most they will do is scan your content, so make it easy for them to do so. Replace your prose with headlines and bullets, so they can quickly run their eye over the details and still get an accurate picture of the opportunity.

Rule #5
Get Them to Act Even if They Don't Apply

Writing a job posting for passive high caliber candidates is an investment of your time and talent, so make sure you derive a meaningful return on that effort. The optimal response, of course, is an application, but if that doesn't happen, make sure you have a fallback. Offer them two additional ways to act on your ad: give them the ability to refer the opening to a friend or colleague (because top talent know other top talent) and invite them to join your network of contacts so you can keep them informed of other openings in the future.

Unfortunately, most job postings today are a modern medical miracle. They are a cure for insomnia in 500 words or less.

To avoid that outcome, write your job postings using the five rules for seducing top talent. They'll be much more likely to fall for your opening if you do.

A Social Job Posting

Not much has changed with job postings since they first appeared in the early 1990's. Today, they are – as they have always been – information-based ads that are shaped by their ancestors in the classified section of newspapers. What has changed, however, is the people who read job postings. They want a different experience, one that is social as well as informative.

Unfortunately, the Web is filled with poorly written job postings. These recruitment ads are nothing more than position descriptions or print classified ads repurposed online. They may work with the so-called active job seekers, but for talented candidates with choices, they have all of the appeal of a wet blanket on a cold day.

The social job posting, therefore, has two ambitious goals. First, it transforms the traditional posting into an electronic sales brochure – an ad with the persuasive power to convince even the most passive candidate to pay attention. And second, it transforms the employer-centric feel of a traditional posting into a more balanced experience – an ad with a social dimension that includes the reader.

How does it accomplish these goals?

A social job posting draws on the Socratic method to establish a "silent dialogue" between the employer or recruiter and the reader. It is a virtual two-way conversation once removed. In other words, the ad creates an indirect conversation between the two parties by using embedded questions from one to evoke a response from the other.

This more social experience has a number of important benefits:

It increases the engagement of the reader, which is likely to affect passive prospects the most as they are normally the least captivated by conventional job postings.
It produces a more thoughtful response by the reader, which is likely to improve self-selection and reduce the number of unqualified applicants.
It differentiates the organization's employment brand, which is likely to enhance its visibility and stature among high caliber candidates.

In effect, a social job posting has the power to increase the quality of an organization's yield from online recruitment ads and thus the return on its investment in that medium.

The Format & Content of a Social Job Posting

A social job posting is divided into five distinct sections that make up the acronym S-ABC-S. They are:

Summary	What are the key aspects of the vacancy's value proposition in no more than five lines?
Advantages	What will a new hire get to do, learn, and accomplish, with whom with they work and how will they be recognized and rewarded?
Benefits	What tangible and intangible benefits does the organization offer to enhance the employment experience of its workers?
Culture	What aspects of the employer's culture and values will enable the new hire to thrive at their work and make a valued contribution?
Sign-off	What courses of action are offered to the job seeker for their response to the ad?

As different as this format is, what gives the ad its power is its content. It doesn't focus on what's important to employers – requirements and responsibilities – but instead features the motivating factors for the candidate – what's in it for them. In other words, the ad treats the candidate as a consumer and sells them on the employer and its opening.

That approach is then reinforced with the Socratic method. Every three or four paragraphs in each section of the ad, the reader is asked a question that focuses their attention on the content and helps them relate it to themselves.

For example, after describing an employer's team-oriented approach to accomplishing work, the ad might ask:

"Do you find that you perform best when working in a team?"

These questions create a unique and compelling social experience for the reader. They aren't being talked at – as is the case with traditional job postings – but instead are being talked with. They feel as if the employer is engaging them in a discussion and that the purpose of that discussion is to help them determine if the opening is right for them.

The social job posting isn't a silver bullet. It won't change a dreary position into a dream job. It will, however, add a powerful, new dimension to what a job posting does. A social job posting begins to **build the reader's allegiance** to the employer, and as a consequence, dramatically increases their propensity to apply for its opening.

Application Triggers for Passive Prospects

Given the workload of recruiters these days, few have the time to craft a brand new ad for each and every job they post on the Web. And even when a posting gets the attention it deserves, all too often it includes copy invented in the 1950s. The ad will highlight the "requirements and responsibilities" of the job and overlook altogether the content that triggers talented people to apply.

While active job seekers can be and often are top performers, they represent only one-fifth of the workforce. According to the U.S. Bureau of Labor Statistics, at any point in time – even during a recession – just 16 percent of the workforce is actively in transition. If you want to reach and influence the other four-fifths of the working population, therefore, you must write a job posting that will trigger employed people to action.

Why do they need a special trigger? Because unlike active job seekers, employed people have a potent "inherent choice." They don't have to apply for a job; they can stay right where they are. And, if they're at the top of their field, their current employer is doing everything possible to make sure they do. All too frequently, the net result is an indifferent candidate or what most recruiters call the "passive job seeker."

Content that describes the "requirements and responsibilities" of a position is important, but not sufficient to motivate a passive person to apply. What's also necessary is a stimulus – a reason for them to choose to leave their passivity and act. Basically, they must be stimulated to do the one thing human beings most hate to do: *change*.

Change, of course, involves risk and most people are risk averse. So, the only way to persuade someone they should do something different in their career – like apply for a new job – is to trigger a response in them that is more powerful than their fear of change.

The OPFE Formula

There are five such triggers for passive prospects:

Status	Derived from the position, the employer or both.
Security	Based on the track record of the boss, the employer or both.
Sociality	Derived from the values and culture of coworkers, leaders or both.
Standing	Based on the importance of the work, the success of the employer or both.
Rewards	As determined by the practices of the boss and the capacity of the employer.

These factors make up the OPFE Formula for highlighting the Opportunity available to passive prospects and overcoming the Fear that paralyze many of them. Collectively, they can be summarized in two categories of triggers that are powerful enough to counter the perception of risk. The more clearly a job posting features one to leverage the other of these factors, the more likely it is to catch the attention and pique the interest of people who don't want to *change*.

The key to using OPFE effectively is to recognize passive prospects' inherent choice but leverage your organization's inherent strengths. Focus your ad on the advantages of your organization rather than the vulnerabilities of a prospect's current employer. In other words, address the positive you own and avoid the negative you don't. The prospect, in turn, will make the connection from your opportunity to their fear all by themselves.

For example, if your ad describes how the job will position a person to advance in their field (i.e., their standing), a passive prospect will recognize that Opportunity, and if appropriate, also confront their Fear that they are falling behind with their current employer. Similarly, if your ad focuses on the team spirit at your employer (i.e., its sociality), they will see the Opportunity they can derive from that culture, but may also acknowledge their Fear that the more competitive culture of their current employer is hurting them.

In the investment field, actions are often based on a risk-reward calculus. If the potential risk is significantly less than the potential reward, an investor is making a rational decision in acting. Passive prospects perform the same calculus, but in reverse. They see a reward and then consider the risk.

To motivate them, therefore, a job posting must focus on the Opportunity of an opening so a prospect will tap into whatever

Fear they may be feeling about their current position, boss, coworkers or employer. The outcome of that often unconscious deliberation is also a rational decision to act, but in this case it will be to apply for your opening.

Take Your Best Shot First

Passive high caliber talent have the attention span of a gnat. Such peak performers are interested in career advancement opportunities, but they're totally uninterested in reading about them. How can you hang onto them long enough to pique their curiosity about your opening? Take your best shot at the very beginning of your job posting.

Most job postings today start with what the employer wants a new hire to do for it. They're gussied up position descriptions similar to the following actual ad content:

Sales Representatives sought to join XYZ Company's successful sales team.

Currently we are seeking a professional and dedicated Sales Representative with a background in respiratory services, durable medical equipment sales or home medical equipment sales to help us grow our business.

Such ad content may appeal to active job seekers, but it leaves passive prospects cold. People who already have a job – and that's largely the case with passive high caliber talent – don't want to know what an opening can do for the employer; they want to know what it can do for them.

Equally as important, they don't have a lot of patience with an ad making them read six, eight, ten or more paragraphs before it provides that information. They want to know what they want to know fast and right at the start. So, take your best shot first and make it matter to them.

Front Load Your Posting With JECC

Research indicates that only a small set of triggers has the power to motivate a passive prospect into action. These triggers are not the "requirements and responsibilities" of a job – what an employer wants a job seeker to do and be – but rather what it is about the position that could be advantageous to them.

In addition, given their short attention span, that information has to be delivered in the first five lines of a job posting and with language that will catch their attention or pique their curiosity or – best of all – do both. It has to be up front, hard hitting and on target.

The formula for such an introductory paragraph is JECC, where:

J describes why the opening is a dream job for top talent.	Why is it an extraordinary career advancement opportunity for them?
E describes why the organization with the opening is a dream employer for top talent.	What makes it an extraordinary place to work and advance their career?

C̲ indicates the range of compensation the opening provides.	Top performers don't work for money, but do use their paycheck to gauge their career advancement. They won't even consider a job where there isn't a financial advantage for them or even bother to apply for one where they can't determine whether there is.
C̲ indicates the organization's commitment to candidate confidentiality.	Passive, high caliber talent have something to lose by considering another position – their current job – so they need to be explicitly reassured that their privacy will be protected.

Admittedly, it's not easy to write such a paragraph, but its potential impact is worth the effort. It embodies the Golden Rule of Recruiting: *What you do to recruit the best talent will also recruit mediocre talent, but the converse is not true.* If you want your job posting to engage passive high caliber prospects, you have to deliver your content the way they want it. You have to take your best shot first.

NEXT PRACTICES
IN SOCIAL
RECRUITING

The social aspect of recruitment has always been recognized among recruiters … and seldom used by them. Why? Because it takes more time than most recruiters have to perform traditional face-to-face networking effectively. However, what's now called "social recruiting" – using social media and other social capabilities online for talent acquisition – has the potential to solve that dilemma. And yet, social recruiting is not without its own problems. All too often, it too is a time sink and/or fails to deliver the necessary talent.

How can you leverage the power of social recruiting and still work efficiently?

IMPLEMENT THE FOLLOWING NEXT PRACTICES:
Whom Are We Trying to Socialize?
Post-Social Recruiting
Post-Social Recruiting, Part II
How to Build a Post-Social Corporate Career Center
The Inconvenient Truth of Recruiting

Whom Are We Trying to Socialize?

We live in a world guided by numbers. They tell us which keywords generate the most traffic to our organization's career site, where we're most likely to connect with highly skilled candidates online, and how much it will cost to participate in a career fair for our target demographic. As useful as these metrics are, however, there's another that's far more important and often overlooked. It's the number that tells us whom we should be socializing if we expect to source and recruit top talent.

According to the U.S. Bureau of Labor Statistics, just 16 percent of the workforce is in transition at any point in time. They are the people we typically describe as "active job seekers." They don't require a lot of convincing to visit our organizational career sites, they flock to job boards and social media sites by the millions, and they steadfastly endure even the most obtuse application forms on our applicant tracking systems.

To put it bluntly, we don't have to worry about the 16 percent. They're motivated to come to us. It's the other 84 percent of the workforce that represents the greatest potential upside and the greatest challenge for recruiters. It is also the number on which we should always be focused.

Why?

> First, we have a higher probability of acquiring top talent in the 84 percent.

Since it represents over four-fifths of all workers, there are simply more top performers in that group than in the 16 percent. To put it another way, the 84 percent gives us better odds that we'll find the talent for which we're looking.

> Second, the Golden Rule of Recruiting is as true today as it was a decade ago.

It goes like this:

What you do to recruit the best talent will also recruit mediocre talent, but the converse is not true.

We give ourselves the best chance of acquiring the "A" and "B" level performers our organization needs, if we tailor our social recruiting efforts to the unique goals and attributes of the 84 percent (where there are more top performers). If, on the other hand, we design our strategy for the 16 percent, we'll almost certainly acquire fewer top performers even as we're inundated with a tsunami of applicants.

The 84 Percent Solution

The 84 percent solution in a social recruiting strategy recognizes that individuals in that group:

are NOT actively looking for a job; and
do NOT think of themselves as a job seeker.

Therefore, every aspect of the candidate experience is designed to convince them that the organization understands and respects those defining attributes.

For example, the recruitment ads that an organization posts on its Facebook page or in its LinkedIn group should be written to describe (and sell) **a career advancement opportunity**, not a job. They should provide as much information about its values and culture as they do about the opening's work objectives and standards.

Similarly, visitors to the organization's Web site should be directed to its online career center with a term such as "Careers," rather than "Employment" or Jobs". And, once in that area, they should be addressed with an inclusive term such as "candidate," rather than "job seeker."

Finally, because the 84 percent are the quintessential "passive" prospects, it's unlikely that they will be drawn to an online career center by jobs alone. Therefore, the content in that area should also include career advancement features and information. These might include:

Blogs written by employees on developments in their field.

The transcripts of employee presentations at professional conferences.
Links to important news stories about the workplace and business.

We should, of course, search 100 percent of the workforce when recruiting. The focus of our efforts, however, should be on the 84 percent who are not actively looking for a job. They are our most important number because they are the candidates who will optimize our yield of top talent.

Post-Social Recruiting

For the past five years, social recruiting has primarily been implemented in two ways: data mining pools of talent and networking with prospective candidates at social media sites. While such techniques will continue to be important, the thrust of social recruiting in the future will shift to a far different kind of activity: *building and leveraging individual allegiance at employer sites.* It's the next phase in the War for the Best Talent – the era of post-social recruiting.

The current incarnation of social recruiting has been stimulated and structured by social media sites. The way we socialize with candidates is governed by the format, functionality and focus of LinkedIn, Facebook and Twitter. These sites enable us to promote our brands, advertise to and connect with large pools of professionals in a wide range of industries.

These interactions have effectively defined social recruiting as a fleeting and thoroughly functional relationship. Basically, we're saying to prospects: "Hey, we're a buyer of talent, you're a seller of talent, let's do a deal." While it isn't the most alluring of propositions, the fact that it is aimed at a cohort of the workforce not easily reached by other media – so-called passive job seekers – has made it an important addition to our recruiting capabilities.

The word "social," however, means something very different from fleeting and functional relationships. Dictionary.com defines the term as "pertaining to, devoted to, or characterized by friendly companionship or relations: a social club." Translated for our purposes, *it is the creation and ongoing development of individual allegiance*. On the one hand, that's post-social, at least as we have to this point understood and implemented social recruiting. And on the other, it is truly social if we intend to use social technology on a large enough scale to address more than one-off requirements.

Post-social recruiting means interactions with prospects, candidates and applicants that make them feel at home with and thus committed to an organization. It gives employers a way to forge an enduring bond – a psychological rather than simply an electronic connection – with select talent populations.

Why is it the future of social recruiting? Because of the past. In the early 1990s, economic conditions and competition forced employers to change the way they dealt with employees. They could no longer afford the expensive overhead of managing workers' careers, so they jettisoned both the career ladder and the gold watch. They still employed those workers, of course, but each person was on their own when it came to managing their career.

In the two decades since then, individual workers have had no place to hang their career hat. No homestead where they can get the practical and psychological support they need and deserve. Professional societies and associations have long served that purpose for a person's field of work, but nothing has existed for a person's career.

And now, the potential exists to correct that situation and, in the process, create a formidable, new talent acquisition strategy. Post-social recruiting involves using social technology to cre-ate true career communities or homesteads – not today's posers that are actually databases of candidates – without the expensive overhead of traditional corporate career support. These virtual "careersteads" nurture allegiance among talented workers and that bond, in turn, transforms them into genuine employment prospects.

Careersteading for Talent

A post-social community is not a network of active or passive job seekers. It is not a one-off interaction on a social media site to fill a specific opening. Rather, a careerstead is a fixed and reliable destination – a homestead – that employers establish for and with prospects (i.e., people who haven't even expressed an interest in working for an organization) as well as with candidates and applicants.

Its purpose is not near term sourcing, but rather, long term interactions that help to promote the career success of those who participate. That effort, in turn, develops and sustains *individual allegiance*, and it's that bond which generates recruiting benefits – in the near term as well as down the road.

These benefits include:

> **A heightened viral effect,** because those who participate feel safe and supported enough to tell their peers about the community. The allegiance community members feel toward the organization encourages them to champion participation in that community to others in their field; and

A heightened employment propensity, because those who participate feel as if the organization has their best interests at heart. The allegiance of community members encourages them to work for the organization as many times as possible throughout their career. They may leave to go to other organizations from time-to-time, but their loyalty will always be to their homestead.

In effect, a careerstead is a highly focused, self-sustaining talent generator that exclusively serves the recruiting interests of a single employer.

How do you create such a community? Not with questions and answers on a Facebook page. And, not with job postings in a LinkedIn group or on a Twitter feed. No, the only way to establish a true careerstead – one that scales the power of social technology to address all or most of an organization's talent requirements – is by breaking all the rules we've learned to date about social recruiting. I'll talk more about that in Post-Social Recruiting, Part II.

Post-Social Recruiting, Part II

As I explained in my last essay, post-social recruiting involves using social technology to create true career communities without the expensive overhead of traditional corporate career support. Unlike candidate databases and networks, these virtual "careersteads" nurture allegiance among talented workers and that bond, in turn, transforms them into genuine and long-term employment prospects.

A careerstead advances an organization's recruiting by providing two important benefits:

A heightened viral effect because the allegiance community members feel toward the organization encourages them to champion participation in that community to others in their field thereby expanding the talent the organization can reach; and

A heightened employment propensity because the allegiance of community members encourages them to work for the organization as many times as possible throughout their career thereby deepening its talent bench.

So, how do you create a careerstead? Not with questions and answers on your organization's Facebook page. And, not with job postings in a LinkedIn group or on a Twitter feed. No, the only way to establish a true careerstead – one that scales the power of social technology to address all or most of your organization's talent requirements – is by breaking all the rules you've learned to date about social recruiting.

Unlike the fleeting and thoroughly functional relationships of conventional social recruiting, a careerstead establishes, maintains and nurtures on-going and entirely altruistic interactions with talented people, whether they are applicants or not. These interactions are designed to promote each person's success by providing them with the information and assistance they need for effective *career self-management*. That support, in turn, builds a psychological connection or individual allegiance to the organization with the resulting sourcing and recruiting benefits.

Erecting a Careerstead

A careerstead may have a presence on the Web as a stand-alone destination on your organization's corporate Web-site or, less optimally, within its online area or page for job seekers. That physical manifestation, however, does not create the allegiance which gives a careerstead its recruiting power. Only social messaging – a consistent engagement using the right content delivered in the right way – can do that.

There are only two kinds of content capable of building allegiance among top talent. One addresses the dynamics and changes in a person's specific career field while the other focuses on more general but still useful career (not job search) strategies and tactics. While either will contribute to a prospect's allegiance, publishing both provides the strongest and most enduring bond. The former enables a person to understand what it takes to advance in their field, while the latter ensures they know the best methods for doing so.

There is usually broad agreement among those in a specific career field about what constitutes the most useful information and insights for individual advancement. In some fields, it's codified as the requirements for certification, and in others, it's presented in the publications of a professional society or trade association.

What constitutes the most useful career information in those fields, however, is less well understood. Through no fault of their own, most workers today lack any awareness of the body of knowledge and set of skills involved in managing their own career. For the past 75 years or more, American colleges and universities have been teaching their students a great deal about specific fields of study, but absolutely nothing about how to make a career in those fields. And, the best way to remediate that situation is with an ongoing education in the principles and practices of effective career self-management.

Where can you obtain such a curriculum? A Google search of the term "career self-management" yields over 119,000,000 results, so the challenge isn't finding content, but determining which content is best. Your safest bet is to use content developed by professional career counselors and coaches or that found in published workbooks and guides.

Content alone, however, is insufficient to engage the participants in your careerstead. That content must also be delivered without the pedantic tone of many online learning experiences. So, conclude each communication with a question and an invitation. The question should be designed to encourage your careersteaders to discuss the real world implications of what they are learning, while the invitation should encourage them to have that discussion in a blog, online discussion forum or listserv located on your careerstead. This discussion should be a carefully moderated interaction that reinforces your organization's role as the source of career expertise and support for participants.

While there are any number of other features a careerstead might offer to individuals, it should, of course, also provide easy access to the organization's available career opportunities. This listing should not intrude on the social aspect of the community, but instead be positioned as a natural extension of the organization's efforts to promote the success of its members.

A careerstead recognizes the inherent uncertainty of today's workplace and leverages it into a powerful recruiting strategy. Yes, it requires an adjustment to traditional staffing assignments within the recruiting team, but the return on that change – both in the short as well as the long term – is potentially significant. Indeed, because it generates a psychological as well as an electronic connection – a unique form of individual allegiance – a careerstead provides both privileged access to top talent and a formidable barrier to the competition for it.

How to Build a Post-Social Corporate Career Center

Today's typical corporate career site has all of the appeal of a brick. Its one-off, transactional focus may be tolerated by active job seekers, but for high caliber, passive prospects, it's an invitation to spend time elsewhere. Those hard-to-recruit individuals have choices, so they demand a very different kind of experience, one that only a post-social career center can provide.

Unlike conventional corporate career sites, a post-social career center is designed to create and sustain a bond with employment candidates. Instead of relying solely on a technological connection, it reinforces that inanimate contact with a psychological connection. It promotes an individual's career success rather than the organization and its open jobs. In effect, a post-social career center is a "careerstead" – a homestead for individual careers – rather than an in-your-face recruitment advertising platform.

This interaction has several aspects that make it particularly appealing to talented workers.

First, it focuses on them rather than on the employer.

It is about their aspirations and success, not some opening's requirements and responsibilities.

> **Second, it is enduring rather than situational.**

It is always there for them and continues on regardless of a person's employment status at any point in time.

> **Third, it is a helpful resource rather than a hard sell.**

It provides information and insights they can use to advance their career, whether or not they've applied for a particular opening.

Those attributes are so rare, so outside the norm of what talented people experience at today's corporate career sites, they forge an allegiance to the organization that has two extraordinary sourcing and recruiting benefits:

> **A heightened viral effect,** because those who experience the site are so intrigued and pleased with what happens to them, they want to tell their peers about it; and

> **A heightened employment propensity,** because those who experience the site feel as if the organization has their best interests at heart.

A careerstead attracts more high caliber talent than conventional corporate career sites and transforms more of those visitors into applicants. And, in this era of tight budgets, there's no better return on an organization's investment in online talent acquisition.

The Features & Functionality of a Careerstead

An online career center that operates as a careerstead provides all of the content and capabilities typically offered active job seekers as well as three unique aspects that are especially appealing to passive high caliber talent:

A way of organizing content so visitors don't feel as if they're "generic candidates;"
The publication of high quality content for successful career self-management; and
The ability to network with their peers and the employer's top employees.

Let's take a brief look at each of them.

Avoiding the Generic Candidate Syndrome

The content at most conventional corporate career sites is written as if it's appropriate for and useful to all candidates. In truth, however, a salesperson is likely to have very different interests and questions than a finance professional, and a finance professional, in turn, is likely to have a different outlook than an IT professional. Therefore, to ensure that each candidate feels as if they are being treated as *an individual* and in a way that actually serves their needs, the site's content must be:

(a) organized into separate channels for each of the major demographics an employer recruits; and	(b) tailored to their particular perspective and information needs.

For example, each of the channels would describe what it's like to work as an employee in an organization in a particular field – sales, finance, IT and so on – and might include testimonials from current employees in that field to add human interest and/or conference presentations or publications by those employees to add credibility.

Adding Career Self-Management Content

The content on most corporate career sites focuses on providing information for active job seekers. According to the U.S. Bureau of Labor Statistics, however, just 16 percent of the American workforce is in transition at any time. In other words, current career site content is irrelevant to four-fifths of all prospective visitors to a site. Therefore, to ensure those non-job seekers are engaged and helped by what they find on a site, it must:

(a) provide the knowledge and skills required for successfully managing a *career* in today's turbulent economy; and	(b) help them deal with the issues and challenges that can derail a career (e.g., a biased boss, gaps in their expertise).

For example, the site might offer a self-study curriculum in career self-management that would keep people coming back to the site continuously and offer assessments and quizzes that could help them gauge their current status in the workplace and the health of their career.

Creating a Career Conversation

Most of today's corporate career sites subject their visitors to a "unilogue," a one-sided conversation. The sites do all the talking (through dense, unexciting prose) and candidates are expected to sit back and take it. Of course, most of the best prospects don't. What they want is *a dialogue* both with those who would be their colleagues if they went to work with the organization and, equally as important, with their peers. Therefore, to ensure that top talent has the kind of professional conversation that will attract and retain their interest, a site must provide:

(a) the functionality for an open but moderated discussion of occupational and industry topics; and	(b) a mechanism for interacting with employees in a representative range of career fields.

For example, the organization might set up a program which enables top employees to compete for a short (e.g., 3 month) assignment blogging on the site about what it's like to work for the organization in their field. Participation could be promoted by providing selectees with a bump in their next performance appraisal score, a monetary reward or both.

The best talent are almost always employed. To recruit them, therefore, we have to convince them to do the one thing we humans most hate to do: *change*. Only a post-social online career center can create the psychological connection that predisposes them to do so.

The Inconvenient Truth of Recruiting

Here's the inconvenient truth of recruiting: we reject 99 percent (or more) of our job applicants. In today's economy, there are more often than not far more people vying for our openings than we can possibly hire. So, the question is: will we disappoint those we turn down or will we give them a reason to come back and try again?

The answer to that question turns on our assessment of the candidates who are not selected for the opening to which they apply. While some organizations treasure these individuals as "runners up," many others see them as "rejects" and not worthy of further consideration.

If you have any doubt about that, consider this: an organization's resume database (the place where all those non-selectees reside) doesn't even make it onto the list of external hire sources reported in the latest CareerXroads survey. It's somewhere below the last identified source – walk-ins – which produces just eight-tenths of one percent of all new hires.

Whatever we may say about previous applicants – and no organization consciously dismisses them – our behavior suggests an underlying and pernicious bias: we don't think of the 99 percent as prime candidates. Even the person who was the runner up for the job to which they applied and the individual who turned down our offer because the timing wasn't right are tossed into an undifferentiated database and, from then on, ignored.

And, that kind of behavior has real consequences. When candidates are ignored, they are inevitably disappointed. In us and our organization. And, widespread disappointment among candidates can hurt our employer's brand and ultimately our talent yield. It can complicate, frustrate and even devastate our ability to hire top performers.

Yes, budgets are tight and recruiters are stretched to the limit just keeping up with current openings, but this is a situation which cannot be ignored. We must start paying more attention to the 99 percent. The question, of course, is how to do so within the constraints with which we work.

A Post-Social Solution for the 99 Percent

For most employers, the 99 percent is composed of two cohorts of the workforce:

those who have previously applied and whose resume or profile is now archived in a resume database; and	those who have yet to apply and to experience the disappointment of not being selected.

Now, in a perfect world, a strategy would be tailored to the different circumstances of each group. In today's time and resource constrained environment, however, that's simply not feasible. So, the better approach is to focus on an attribute shared by most of the individuals in both of those groups.

What is that attribute? They all want to be more successful in their career. So, that's what we should help them do. If we can't give them a job, we can at least give them the information that will help them advance in their career.

How do we do that? Re-imagine our organization's online destination for candidates. Most companies and staffing firms call that area a "career site" or "career page." It's not. In the vast majority of cases, it's simply a place for informing job seekers and processing their applications.

While what we tell them about our culture, values, benefits and opportunities is important, it isn't enough. Ultimately, it will only matter to the 1 percent who are actually selected for a job with the organization. For the other 99 percent, it might as well be a user's manual for sharpening quill pens. Basically, it has no value at all to or for them.

To pay attention to the 99 percent, we have to post information and provide features that will enable them to upgrade their credentials and advance themselves in their profession, craft or trade (even if we don't hire them).

For example, we might set up a "candidate university" on our site that offered:

The videos of conference presentations and the white papers written by our organization's current employees;	Republished articles from the journals of select professional societies with a link back to the association's site to help it capture new members; and	A training program in the principles and practices of career self-management that would enable them to be a stronger candidate for our organization's future openings.

For 99 percent of all applicants, the candidate experience doesn't end once a person has been selected for an opening. It continues on. And, that long experiential tail is just as important – and maybe more given the numbers involved –as what we do to and for candidates before a hire is made. No commercial organization can survive if it disappoints the majority of its prospective customers, and no recruiting organization can either.

NEXT PRACTICES
IN CANDIDATE ENGAGEMENT

Top talent are busy and driven people. They are almost always employed and have a lot of responsibility at work. They are determined to perform at their peak and to maximize the contribution they make on-the-job. They are the quintessential "A" or "B" level employee and, for that reason, they are also the person every recruiter seeks. The very attributes that make them so appealing, however, also make them incredibly difficult to recruit. They are not focused on the job market or even interested in it. They are, in short. the ultra-distracted candidate.

How can you overcome the distraction of top talent and effectively engage them?

IMPLEMENT THE FOLLOWING NEXT PRACTICES:
Become a Talent Whisperer
What 11/22/63 Can Teach Recruiters
Deadlines vs. Lifelines
Treat Your Talent Pipeline as a Rest Stop
Use the Socratic Method in Candidate Email

Become a Talent Whisperer

Talent is hard to find, to be sure, but talking to talent effectively is even harder to do. Not only must we convince superior performers of our organization's value proposition, but in today's Web-centric world, we have to accomplish that feat in writing and in the blink of an eye. The key to success, therefore, is to learn and practice the art of "talent whispering."

A whisperer has been defined as "someone who possesses an extraordinary – highly developed – skill at being able to read and understand communication at a deep 'unspoken' level." They are empathetic people who know how to interact with others in order to catch their attention, engage their interest and influence their behavior.

Now, some will tell you that whispering is an inherent trait. You're either born with it or you aren't. While there are undoubtedly natural born whisperers, however, the fact that whispering is a skill means that it can be learned. In other words, all of us have the potential to be a whisperer, and every recruiter is a talent whisperer waiting to happen.

Why bother? Because mediocre talent will listen to anybody. The best talent will not. Top performers are much more discriminating in their listening habits.

A talent whisperer, therefore, is a recruiter who can quickly and effectively connect with candidates who typically shut out everyone else. They know what to say and how to say it so that these high value prospects can't help themselves; they are compelled to take note of and respond to the message.

An Extraordinary Point of View

To become a talent whisperer, a recruiter must first adopt an extraordinary point of view. While they work for their employer and always serve its best interests, they must re-imagine themselves as "a healer of candidates." They must believe that their job is to help working men and women succeed.

Adopting that perspective differentiates them among the legions of recruiters who contact top talent. More importantly, it also reassures each candidate that they will be treated honestly, fairly and respectfully. They know that the recruiter works for his or her employer, but they sense that the recruiter's interest is in them.

Admittedly, that notion contradicts the conventional view that an employer is best served by doing what's best for the employer. It posits, instead, that an employer is best served by doing what's best for its employment prospects.

That contradiction does make sense, however, because talented people are peak performers. Their contribution exceeds the norm and, frequently, also raises the performance of everyone else in the organization. So, by serving the best interests of top talent, a recruiter can bring more of that kind of performer into the organization, and that outcome, in turn, serves the best interests of the employer.

How do you convince talented people that you are there for them? With empathy– the ability to understand and share the feelings of others.

A talent whisperer puts every word, every phrase, every bit of information in an email, InMail or other online communication through a single, pass-fail test to determine if it is appropriate for use in an interaction with a candidate. That test is composed of a single axiom we all learn as kids, but all too often, forget as adults: the Golden Rule. A talent whisperer is a recruiter who puts him or herself in candidates' shoes and speaks to them as they would like to be spoken to in such circumstances.

Research has found that fifty percent of all online communications are misunderstood. In most cases, it's the tone of messages that is misconstrued, and the consequences can be significant. Recipients are left confused, disaffected or even insulted, and the sender is left empty-handed. For high caliber prospects, in particular, careless word choice or awkward phrasing can inadvertently convey a tone of disrespect, haughtiness or indifference that causes them to hit the Delete button without a second thought.

How can you prevent such misunderstandings? Whisper first to your colleagues. Marketing and corporate communications professionals routinely test their communications with focus groups. You should test yours as well, but do so with coworkers in the department or unit for which you're recruiting. They have the right perspective to evaluate the clarity and impact of your messages.

So, if you want passive, high caliber talent to pay attention to you, whisper to them. Empathize with them. Speak to them as if you were speaking to yourself. And, then, be even kinder.

What 11/22/63 Can Teach Recruiters

Stephen King once wrote a book called *11/22/63*. It's a time-travel story about a man who ventures back to that date – the day President John F. Kennedy was assassinated. His mission is to change the past, to prevent the crime, and thus reshape the world he and we know. It's a fascinating yarn, but just as important, the truth it reveals about resetting ourselves offers a useful lesson for recruiters.

The time traveler is a high school English teacher who befriends an old man with an astonishing secret. He owns a greasy spoon diner that holds a portal to the past. The old man is dying of cancer so he extracts a promise from the teacher. He agrees to travel back in time and avert one of the most shocking crimes of the 20th Century – the murder of a young president and the obliteration of the hope he inspired.

The time travel portal, however, is a fickle passage and deposits the teacher in 1958, over three years before his appointed date with destiny. As he awaits that moment, he prevents a heinous crime he knows will be committed (thanks to his foreknowledge of the past), runs afoul of a bookie because he wins too much (thanks again to his foreknowledge of the past) and meets the love of his life (for which he is totally unprepared because she's not in his future unless he changes the past). Get it?

Throughout it all, he steadily and stealthily prepares for his assignment. And, it's that effort which teaches him King's view of the past. As the author sees it, what's over and done cannot be done over. Or, as he says, the past is "obdurate." It stubbornly refuses to change. The teacher is deeply committed to his mission, but the past conjures up situations and people to keep him from accomplishing his goal.

You'll have to read the book to see how it all turns out. The nature of the past, however, is an important insight for recruiters. Why? Because undoing some of the events in our past would do some good. While we are obviously innocent of any crime, we have on occasion acted in ways that would benefit from correction. None of us is perfect, so getting a second chance could have a very positive impact.

Revisiting the Past to Undo It

There are, of course, at least two versions of the past for those of us in the field of recruiting. There is our version – the way we see the events that took place – and there is the version of candidates – their view of what happened, particularly to them.

While we often saw terribly written resumes, totally unqualified applicants and atrociously unprepared interviewees, our applicants saw something else entirely. And, while our view is important and likely the most accurate, it is the view of those candidates that will determine the caliber of our organization's employment brand and ultimately our success in the War for the Best Talent.

So, what is the prevailing view of applicants? Survey after survey confirms that they believe they have been mistreated and disrespected by employers and recruiters. As they see it, they submit resumes that disappear into a black hole, they are thrown into a process that feels like quicksand, and they are interviewed by hiring managers with the social skills of a brick.

The past they know is discourteous, demoralizing and all too often demeaning. But, it is not obdurate. Memories are malleable. We can change applicants' view of the past by making the present a more engaging and respectful experience.

How do we accomplish that?

By transforming the static database of electronic records in our applicant tracking system into a dynamic community of people. By devoting the same time and effort we now invest in networking with strangers on social media sites to building allegiance among prospects who have already expressed an interest in employment with our organization. No less important, as many of those records are several years old, they are likely to describe individuals who have taken a job elsewhere, and are now the quintessential "passive job seeker" – the very kind of talent for which most organizations are searching.

What should we communicate? There is a wide range of possible topics, including:

News about the organization's successes (e.g., innovative products or services that have been introduced, new facilities that have been opened);
News about the successes of individual employees (e.g., awards they have received from professional societies, degrees they have earned from academic institutions);

Links to posted white papers and conference presentations by the organization's employees; and

Information about the organization's social and community activities (e.g., corporate blood drives, employees working on a local Habitat for Humanity).

Whatever is communicated, however, the key is continuity. Be in touch with past applicants regularly in the present.

Many employers now have hundreds of thousands of resumes in computer storage. Unfortunately, getting to that point was probably an unpleasant experience for many of the applicants behind those documents. Their sense of the past, however, can be reset. Not by traveling back in time, but by moving forward in the present with the simple act of paying attention to them on a regular basis and in a collegial and respectful way.

Deadlines vs. Lifelines

Recruiters live in a world defined by deadlines. Requisitions must be filled by a certain date, so sourcing, interviews, and reference checks have to be completed by earlier ones. Meeting those deadlines, however, can cause us to overlook a different kind of line, one that is especially important to our candidates. I call them "lifelines."

A lifeline isn't defined by time. It is determined, instead, by quality. It is a measure of the caliber of the interaction we have with our candidates. If we miss a deadline, we have failed to accomplish a certain task within a certain time. If we miss a lifeline, we have failed to provide a certain kind of experience for a certain kind of candidate.

Why is that important? Because the quality of our candidates' experience determines the quality of our new hires.

We hear people say "garbage in, garbage out" to describe the need for good data in our decision-making. The same is true with our recruiting. Only for us, it's better expressed as "quality in, quality out."

What is a quality experience and to whom should we provide it?

The lifeline experience is characterized by empathy. It occurs when we acknowledge the bond that joins us all as people. We are not indifferent machines or processes, but are, instead, men and women who just happen to be on different sides of the workplace. Our lives may be different, but our life – our humanity – is identical.

I realize that may be a bit too metaphysical for some, so consider this. One of the earliest lessons we are taught as kids is the Golden Rule. It's as simple as it is profound. Do unto others as you would have them to do unto you. Or, to put it another way, always offer others a lifeline because, at some point, we may need one too.

To Whom Should We Offer a Lifeline?

Offering a lifeline takes time and effort, so to whom should we extend one?

In a world dominated by deadlines and tight resources, the most common strategy is now to do less with less. As the oft heard refrain goes, "we get hundreds, sometimes thousands of applicants for each of our openings, and we simply don't have the time to give each of them individual attention." Or to put it more bluntly, our deadlines trump our lifelines.

What's the alternative to such a strategy? We should give lifelines equal priority with deadlines. We should offer a lifeline to every single candidate.

For every dollar we spend on sourcing new prospects, we should spend a commensurate dollar empathizing with those who have already applied. For every hour we invest in using social media to reach out to strangers, we should invest the same commitment in practicing the Golden Rule with those who've already expressed an interest in our openings. For every career fair we attend to connect with unknown candidates, we should hold a "lifefair" with those we have already met in our ATS database.

How will that strategy impact our performance, especially as it's perceived by those hiring managers who think recruiting is as simple as shooting fish in a barrel?

Meeting deadlines gets our job done. Forging lifelines gets our job done well. Timing is important to our customers, to be sure, but in a highly competitive global marketplace, quality of hire is more important. It enables hiring managers to optimize their performance. And, if we give them that outcome, they'll give us the credit we deserve.

Treat Your Talent Pipeline as a Rest Stop

What's the number one problem with today's talent pipe-lines? Attrition. According to research, the number of people bailing out of recruiter-built networks typically reaches forty percent or more each year. Given the time and effort required to load a pipeline, that's a huge loss for any organization. What's the solution? Re-imagining the purpose of your pipeline.

Unfortunately, for many organizations, a talent pipeline is simply a resume database by another name. Oh sure, today's pipelines are built on social media sites like Facebook or LinkedIn, but there's very little social activity actually going on. In fact, if there's any communications at all with the people in the pipeline, it's either repurposed job postings or hard sell promotions designed to drive traffic to the organization's Web-site (and its job postings).

Which begs the question: just what is the purpose of a talent pipeline? Is it simply a passageway way for moving candidates from a passive to an active candidate state? Or, is the goal some-thing else altogether? Is a talent pipeline not a pipeline at all, but instead, a virtual rest stop for prospective employees?

Sure, you build talent pipelines to help fill your organiza-tion's current and future openings, but the goal of those pipelines is the experience they provide to individuals who have choices in the workplace. High caliber performers are almost always employed, so to recruit them, you must get them to do the one

NEXT PRACTICES

thing we humans most hate to do: *change*. You have to get them to leave their current employer, turn down offers from other employers, and accept the position you're trying to fill for your employer.

That outcome simply will not occur with repurposed job postings and hard sell promotions. In fact, research indicates that the single best trigger for motivating change among passive, high caliber candidates isn't requirements and responsibilities, but reality – a reality they have the time to recognize and appreciate.

The best talent wants to know what it's really like to work in your organization. Before they will even consider a job, they need to have a sense of what their employment experience will be like. To put it more bluntly, they must be assured that their personality and principles are aligned with the organization's culture and values so they will be comfortable in its work environment and, able to continue their career success by performing at their peak.

Offering a Glimpse of Reality

Talking about an organization's work culture and values is the conventional way of presenting its employment brand. That's what happens on most corporate career sites and on Facebook pages and in LinkedIn groups. Candidates are proselytized with carefully tested tag lines and peer testimonials.

This advertising-based approach doesn't influence the best talent. The only way to get them to make a change is to treat them as *proto-employees*. They have to believe that an organization already sees them as "members of the family." Why? Because doing so enables them to experience what it's like to be employed by that organization – to get a taste of reality.

How do you create this proto-employee experience?

That's the power and promise of talent pipelines. They are the perfect vehicle for simulating an organization's employment culture and values. First, however, the organization must give its pipeline participants the space to recognize and appreciate that reality. It does so by transforming the pipeline experience into a virtual rest stop, a place where they can get a break from the barrage of recruitment advertising and branding messages countless recruiters have been sending them.

Second, in the quiet space the pipeline provides, an organization's messaging should simulate what it's like to work there. Its messages should act like:

a corporate newsletter and celebrate the accomplishments of the organization's employees (from individual conference presentations to the bowling team's latest victory), the people who would be the pipeline participants' peers if they joined the organization;

a corporate bulletin board and invite them to participate in the kinds of events they would have access to (from attending a company reception during their association's annual conference to joining the company's employees working on a Habitat for Humanity project one weekend), if they were employees of the organization;

a corporate interoffice memo and request their input or assistance with certain organizational challenges and initiatives (from asking for their referrals for key open positions to seeking their input on the company's participation in a municipal ride-sharing program), just as they would be if they worked for the organization.

The term "talent pipeline" is misleading because it conjures up the image of a passageway that enables employers to move candidates from a passive to an active state. That transit-like approach, however, tends to generate high levels of attrition. A more effective alternative, therefore, is to see a talent pipeline as a virtual rest stop. It should be the one place where top talent can be free of recruitment advertising, while being persuaded to change employers by virtually experiencing an organization's employment culture and values.

Use the Socratic Method in Candidate Email

We do it all the time. We find a great prospect for a key opening and send off an email message to start our recruiting conversation. More often than not, however, all that comes back is the sound of silence. The conversation never begins because we haven't structured the message to stimulate a reply. We haven't used the Socratic method.

Email may seem old fashioned in these days of social media, but the research shows it's still the preferred method of online communication. In a survey of 1,100 association members – people who are committed to improving themselves in their profession or what we colloquially call "A" and "B" level performers – the majority reported that they prefer to be contacted by email.

Among all of the survey's respondents, 89 percent said they favored email, while just 8 percent favored social media. And in the cohort of respondents thought to be most committed to social media – those 24 to 34 years of age – the numbers were almost the same. An astonishing 87 percent said they favored email, while 13 percent gave the nod to social media.

Given this preference for email contacts, it's critical that we understand how best to structure such messages to ensure they are successful. What's the definition of success? It has two components:

> First, we must get the prospect to refrain from hitting the Delete button and instead reply to our message; and

> Second, we must pique their interest enough to turn that reply into the first iteration of a conversation.

Getting Prospects to Answer the Mail

The most engaging email messages have three components:

A Personal Greeting.

The email must begin with a salutation that addresses the recipient by name. The best talent abhor being treating as if they are a generic candidate, so such greetings as "Hi There" or "Dear Colleague" are an immediate ticket to the dump. Instead, do your homework, learn the person's first name and begin your message with that. Simple as it sounds, using "Hi Jim" or Hello Jane" helps to establish you as a peer rather than yet another vendor trying to sell them something.

A Value Statement.

The best talent are never interested in a job, but the majority are almost always on the lookout for a career advancement opportunity. So, don't use a bureaucratic job title or position label to introduce your opening. And, don't use words – such as Requirements and Responsibilities – that only an employer could love. Instead, focus on describing "what's in it for them." Tell them what they will get to do, what they can learn, what they will be able to accomplish, whom they will work with and how they will be recognized and rewarded.

A Socratic Trigger.

Our culture teaches people that it's impolite to ignore a question. So, stimulate a reply by ending your message with one. It won't work with every prospect, of course, but it will induce many to reply to your first message and then to every message after that. In your first message, keep your value statement short and sign off by asking if they would like to know more. Then, in subsequent messages, add more detail and ask them if such an opportunity would be right for them at this point in their career or, if they feel as if their current job lacks such challenge and rewards. And, then, keep asking until they hear what they need in order to apply.

This iterative messaging based on questions from you and answers from the prospect is a version of the Socratic method. It educates the message recipient by getting them to tell you what they want (or need) to know. As a result, it transforms the interaction from a sales pitch into a quasi-counseling or coaching experience that will help them see your opening as an opportunity they can't pass up.

NEXT PRACTICES
IN OPTIMIZING
THE CANDIDATE
EXPERIENCE

What kind of experience do you most enjoy when traveling by air: the crowded and overheated seating area at the departure gate or the clean and quiet waiting rooms of the airline clubs? It's the choice that's really no choice at all. And, it's the principal reason why so many employers are now trying to improve the caliber of the experience they provide to candidates. Just as travelers have a choice in airlines, the best talent have a choice in employers, and more often than not, they'll pick the one that treats them best during the recruiting process.

How can you optimize the candidate experience in your recruiting process?

IMPLEMENT THE FOLLOWING NEXT PRACTICES:
Keep Your Promise
The Most Unpopular Term in the Job Market
The Hated Generic Candidate
The Hunger Games of Recruitment
Employers (Inadvertently) Behaving Badly

Keep Your Promise

The best candidates have choices. Most are employed and those who aren't receive a continuous stream of offers from recruiters. How can you differentiate your organization from the herd and your opening from the others that are available? Optimize the candidate experience in your recruiting process by making a promise and then keeping it.

Recruiting the best talent is an exercise in stimulating irrational behavior. Because most top performers are already employed, you have to persuade them to do something they don't want to do – *change*. You must convince them to move from the devil they know (their current employer, boss and commute) to the devil they don't know (your employer, a new boss and a different commute).

What would induce them to take such a crazy (from their perspective) action? You have to make the right promise and then deliver on it. Those two steps are the single best way to optimize the candidate experience. And, an optimal candidate experience is the single best way to pry reluctant talent out of another organization.

The best talent share a similar aspiration: they want to be the best they can be in their profession, craft or trade. Whether they are nurses, accounts payable clerks or salespeople, they are driven to express and experience as much of their talent – their innate capacity for excellence – as they can at work.

For that reason, they are always looking for a "career advancement opportunity," even when they are happily employed. They define such an opportunity as a work experience – a specific job inside a specific organization – that will enable them to perform at their peak. What they want from a prospective employer, therefore, is a commitment to provide just that kind of reality.

Shopping for Employers

Top performers aren't motivated by the requirements and responsibilities of a job. Instead, they want to know what it's like to work in an organization and whether that experience will aid and abet their quest to excel.

Therefore, step one in optimizing the candidate experience is to develop an employment brand which provides that information. Unlike its kissing cousin among consumer brands, however, an employment brand is not a gimmicky tag line. Rather, it is a statement of values. It defines the culture of an organization. In essence, an employment brand makes a promise: it tells the candidate this is what it will be like if you come to work for our organization.

In today's cynical workplace, however, a promise – even the right promise – is only as good as its credibility. To put it another way, top talent shops for employers the same way they shop for a car. They listen to the promise a vendor makes about its product, but they don't accept their statement as fact. Instead, they "test drive" the product to ensure it's true.

How do candidates test drive an employer? They create a surrogate. They use the organization's recruiting process to gauge its work experience. They believe that the way they are treated as a candidate will reasonably simulate the way they will be treated as an employee.

Therefore, step two in optimizing the candidate experience is to align what you've said about your employer's work experience with what you do in your recruiting process. Every interaction and every communication must stay true to and reinforce what the employment brand promised about the culture and values of the organization.

For example, if your organization's employment brand promises a collegial working environment, use an applicant's visit for an interview to illustrate that attribute. Set aside time at the conclusion of the interview to introduce them to the people who would be their colleagues. And, make those introductions in the cubicle area, offices or lab where they would be working. Give them a feel for the supportive culture they would experience as an employee.

To recruit the best talent, make the right promise and keep it. Create a consistent, integrated portrait of what it's like to work in your organization and then bring that portrait to life through the experience you provide candidates in your recruiting process.

The Most Unpopular Term in the Job Market

Amidst all the talk about optimizing the candidate experience, one topic has been all but ignored. The vocabulary we use has a significant impact on the perceptions of those we are trying to recruit. And, one term, in particular, is widely used, but conveys a message that distresses some prospects and repels many others.

A.S. Byatt once opined that "Vocabularies are crossing circles and loops. We are defined by the lines we choose to cross or to be confined by." Words have meaning, of course – they convey information – but they also elicit responses – they touch nerves – that shape the perceptions of those who read them.

For that reason, the choice of words as much as their definition matters in recruitment. In the minds of the people who visit corporate career sites and read job postings, an employer is defined as much by the words it uses as it is by the information it provides or the practices it follows.

The impression is often unintentional, but it is real and potent nevertheless. And, one term that is now jargon to recruiters but anathema to everyone else on the planet is "job seeker." It says an organization views prospective employees as supplicants for work.

The Active & Passive Interpretation

To put it bluntly, both those who are actively looking for a new job and those who are passive prospects think the term "job seeker" signals an organization that may be prejudiced against them. After all, they read the same news reports that everyone else does – you know, the ones that report on surveys which find an unspecified number of recruiters who now view job seekers as damaged goods.

Those actively in the job market may not be put off by the term – they have no choice – but to them it says the employer may well view them as Losers. Passive prospects, on the other hand, refuse to even acknowledge that the term applies to them and avoid the organizations that use it.

If you have any doubt about that latter point, do a survey of the visitors to your corporate career site. Ask about their employment status, and you'll almost certainly find that the vast majority – 80 to 90 percent – are unemployed. And, yet, according to the U.S. Bureau of Labor Statistics, at any point in time, just 16 percent of the workforce is actively in transition. In other words, your site is plumbing the depths of the small cohort of the population that has no choice and missing out altogether on the much larger cohort of people who do.

How can you redress this situation? Not simply by using different words. To be credible, a change in vocabulary must be more than simply a matter of semantics. It must reflect an organization's culture and values.

> First, change the mindset of your organization to remove any conscious or unconscious bias against a prospective hire because of their employment status.

That means ensuring a more inclusive perspective among hiring managers and receptionists as well as recruiters.

> Second, change the vocabulary on your corporate career site and in your job postings to remove any impression that you view potential applicants as Losers.

Move the term "job seeker" to the metatags for your site's pages where it won't be visible to visitors, but will be seen by search engines and thus preserve your site's ranking. Then, use a non-pejorative term such as "candidate" or "applicant" in its place.

To have a lasting impact on the perception of your organization's employment brand, however, you must do more than simply replace one word with another.

Site visitors and ad readers will certainly notice the difference in your vocabulary – it's such a rarity among employers – but they may not understand why you've made the change. So, also include a visible statement – not one hidden six clicks deep in your site – that affirms your organization's commitment to treating everyone as a valued employment prospect.

Jargon is often criticized for its lack of clarity, but in the case of the term "job seeker," its impact is exactly the opposite. To active and passive candidates alike, it sends a clear (if unintentional) signal that the organization views them as damaged goods, and that impression, in turn, undermines the organization's ability to recruit high caliber talent effectively.

The Hated Generic Candidate

The latest "big idea" in recruiting is to optimize the candidate experience. Pundits everywhere have leaped on the bandwagon to offer this strategy or that technique to make people feel better as they pass through the recruiting process. No doubt, it's all helpful advice. But, sadly, it also ignores the one element that most sours the outlook and interest of potential new hires: our demeaning habit of treating every individual as a generic candidate.

Let's start by taking a secret shopper visit to virtually any employer career site on the Web today. As the first page opens, what do we see? There are tabs leading to a description of the organization and its culture, its benefits, and, of course, its jobs. Occasionally, there might be a tab for recent graduates or diversity candidates, but other than that, it's all mayonnaise.

Just as bad, that indifference to individual differences also has a very transactional feel. It's as if the visitor has landed in a store, and the employer is politely but insistently pushing them to make a purchase. "Buy our employer; a job here will look great on your resume."

Active job seekers may have to tolerate such an experience, but for everybody else, it's an engraved invitation to leave the site. And, everybody else is a very big group. According to the U.S. Bureau of Labor Statistics, at any point in time (including during a recession and tepid recovery), only 16 percent of the workforce is actively in transition. In other words, the candidate experience on most corporate career sites is driving away more than four-fifths of the candidate population.

The Better Experience

What's a better experience? Make the visitor feel as if they've entered a farm, and your sole goal is to make them feel welcome and supported. However, such interactions feel genuine and seem credible only if they occur on an individual and personal level.

Now, when you think about it, that's not so unusual. For example, how do you now expect to be treated as an online consumer? Whether you're visiting the site of your favorite bookstore or shoe boutique, the state-of-the-art in consumer technology has conditioned you to believe that the site should recognize and acknowledge your unique shopping preferences.

The bar is a little lower for career sites, but not much. The best candidates don't (yet) expect you to recognize and acknowledge their unique employment background and objectives, but they do want you to treat them as differentiated people of talent. They've worked hard to establish themselves as finance, sales, nursing, information technology, human resource and other kinds of professionals. They don't think it's asking too much, therefore, for you to respect that effort by NOT treating them as generic candidates.

Getting Past Generic

There are many steps you can take to avoid a generic candidate experience on your employer's career site. Among the most important, however, are two that will signal your respect for the key differences among persons of talent. They acknowledge each individual's acquisition of expertise in a particular occupation and their experience applying that knowledge at work.

Step 1

Set up separate channels or areas on your career site for each of the major occupational fields for which you recruit.

Instead of providing an experience where they are directed to visit the department or divisions of your company – distinctions that mean nothing to them – organize your site to give each visitor an area that's been set aside just for them and their peers. Make them feel as if they have a "career home" on your site because you've set aside and labeled special areas for IT, HR, Sales, Marketing and other professionals.

Step 2

Tailor the content in each occupation's channel to the unique aspirations, values and vocabulary of its members.

Describe the unique career path options, work style (e.g., team-based or individual initiative), and rewards for those in that occupation in your organization. Then, support those claims with peer testimonials that are written by your employer's current workers in each field and which describe their actual day-to-day work experience.

No one likes to be treated as one of the herd. To make sure your employer's career site doesn't inadvertently give candidates exactly that kind of experience, transform it from a store to a farm and shift its content from generic to occupation specific information.

Offer Top Talent Career Security

The War for Talent has now defined the recruiting field for a quarter century. While there has been much commentary about optimizing the candidate experience and building organizational cultures of excellence, the principal tactics in this war have been financial. We have paid top talent more to get them in the door and paid them even more to hang onto them. Both were short-sighted.

According to data from SHRM, employers apparently believe they can buy the commitment of high performers. It compiled two sets of data – one from 2004, well before the last recession, and the other from 2008, right in the middle of the downturn. Here's what the data show: before the recession, 61 percent of employers were paying hiring bonuses to lure top talent in the door. In 2008, in the heart of the deepest economic catastrophe since the Great Depression, that figure had increased to 70 percent. Similarly, in 2004, 27 percent of employers were paying retention bonuses to hang onto their talent, and in 2008, that number had grown to 38 percent of employers.

We may talk about all of the other tactics we employ to recruit the best and brightest, but when push comes to shove, we fall back on money. Even in the most difficult economic environments, we pony up to pay more for those with hard-to-find skills and those who are superior performers.

What's wrong with that strategy? The debate goes on, of

course, about whether top talent is, in fact, motivated by money. There are studies that demonstrate they are and studies which just as convincingly, show they aren't. For my part, I believe top talent uses money not as a goal, but as a gauge. It is the single best way for them to measure whether or not they are advancing in their careers, and that growth is their ultimate objective.

But, here's the problem with making financial tactics a key element of your recruiting strategy: Two times out of three, it sets you up for failure. In other words, there are only three potential outcomes with a money strategy and two of them are harmful to your success:

You can't afford to pay top dollar to hire the talent you need so you are always outbid in the marketplace.	You can afford to pay top dollar, but there's always someone else who trumps your bid and lures the talent away.	You can afford to keep paying whatever it takes to hire and hang onto your talent.

The last outcome is, of course, a positive one, but it only exists if you've got unlimited cash or shareholders who don't care about your profit margins.

So, what's the alternative? Focus your value proposition on something other than money. What's that? Well, you can't promise job security, at least not in these uncertain times, but you can offer something top talent will value as much and maybe more: *career security* – a way to achieve their ultimate objective.

Career Security: The Ability to Succeed Successively

Career security is the ability of a person always to be employed and always by an employer of their choice. It acknowledges two realities in today's workplace:

First, in an era of global competition, employer needs and circumstances change much more frequently and unpredictably than ever before.

And second, in an era of global talent, an individual's ability to contribute on-the-job also changes frequently, but with less unpredictability.

While no company can honestly guarantee a person job security, therefore, it can reinforce their career by helping them acquire the knowledge and skills they will need to succeed successively.

How can an employer do that? By teaching employees and candidates alike how to practice effective career self-management.

There are principles and practices for building up the strength, reach and endurance of a career, and sadly, they've been totally ignored by many of our colleges and universities. In effect, those institutions have turned the majority of our workforce into "career idiot savants." They've given their students an in-depth education in a specific field of study, but taught them absolutely nothing about how to make a career with that knowledge.

Faculties work in ivory towers that were erected long before the advent of global competition and talent. They simply don't realize that employers can no longer afford to provide 1950's style career-long guidance and development for their employees. In the 21st century, workers must do it for themselves.

The tragedy, of course, is that almost none of them know how. Talented people are defined by their quest to excel – to be the best they can be in their profession, craft or trade – so they are acutely aware of this shortcoming. Indeed, they more than any others in the workforce recognize the importance of this knowledge. They want to know what they must do and how they must do it in order to achieve a durable, engaging and consistently rewarding career.

Any employer which fills that vacuum will send a powerful and differentiating message to top talent. They are saying: *we care about you and want you to succeed, in our organization and successively wherever else you might be. Yes, of course, we want you to work for us, but we also want you to work where you can grow and excel. That may cause you to leave us at some point, but if you succeed successively, there's a good probability that you'll also come back.*

Admittedly, it takes a brave organization to embark on such a strategy. Because it teaches both candidates and employees to take care of their own careers, it is, in some respects, their emancipation proclamation. However, it is also a unique show of respect for the ultimate goal of those individuals. And for the best talent, there's simply no more powerful and compelling reason to hire on.

Employers (Inadvertently) Behaving Badly

Candidates are people too. And in today's world, people are more social than at any other time in human history. They interact in two different worlds, one real and the other virtual. Treating people poorly during the recruiting process, therefore, can produce a double whammy of harm to an organization's employment brand.

What constitutes bad behavior by an employer? Whatever candidates say it is. That's the recruitment analog to the oldest axiom in business: *the customer is always right.*

So, how do candidates define bad behavior?

While they are irritated by any number of the practices and policies that shape contemporary recruiting processes, their chief complaint – by a very wide margin – is a feeling they get from too many employers. They sense they are being disrespected.

What makes them feel that way? In survey after survey, they identify the causal bad behavior as the "resume black hole." They submit an application and hear absolutely nothing back from the employer. No thank you. No information. Not even an acknowledgement that their resume was received.

We recruiters, of course, have several reasonable explanations for such behavior. These days, we're drowning in resumes and working with historically low levels of both staff and budgets. While that may be wrapped in corporate jargon as "doing more with less,"" it's actual impact is best described as "losing more (talent) with less."

Further, all too often, our technology lets us down. Our applicant tracking systems do generate a response to candidates, but it's written in language only a machine could love. And even if the response does provide a human message, it is distributed in such a way that candidates often never see it.

The Double Dose of Bad News

Here's a truism of the social web. People find their own level. Peers talk to peers. Or to put it more bluntly, the best talent talks to the best talent. So, when we display the kind of behavior that candidates define as bad, the word gets out. And, it gets to the people we least want to hear it.

Worse, candidates also extrapolate. They believe that bad behavior in a recruiting process is a predictor of bad behavior in the workplace. If an organization disrespects its prospective applicants, it is likely to do the same to its employees.

That kind of brand can doom our recruiting efforts no matter how good we are at our job. The best talent has choices, and they will almost always avoid the organization that comes across as a bad employer. Whether they experience its bad behavior themselves or they hear about it from a peer.

So, what should we do?

First, we need to lean on our ATS vendors. We should demand that they provide an auto-responder capable of replying to an unlimited number of applications at any one time. Further, that auto-responder message must permit easy tailoring by recruiters so it both reads as if it was actually written by a human and includes the vocabulary of the specific candidate population being recruited.

Second, once we've acquired the capability for good behavior, we should promote it to the world. We should feature it in every job posting and on our corporate career site, Facebook page, Twitter profile and LinkedIn page

How? By making a two-part statement:

Part One
Our employer's public commitment to acknowledge the receipt of every candidate application.

Part Two
Our employer's public recognition that doing so is a courtesy every candidate deserves.

Then, we have to make sure candidates see us practicing what we preach. Email, however, can often be misclassified by a candidate's email provider, so we must add to our messaging the Internet address (e.g., thankyou@xyx.com) from which our acknowledgement email will come and encourage applicants to add it to their "safe list," so it doesn't get caught in their spam filter.

Assuming the ATS community measures up to its responsibility, that simple assertion will go a long way toward improving the candidate experience and differentiating our employer from those that disrespect applicants. Such delinquents may still attract a lot of applicants, but only we will recruit the best talent.

NEXT PRACTICES
IN YOUR
RECRUITING
CAREER

H ere's a little recognized fact: recruiters have careers too. Most are just as dedicated to their field, just as determined to perform at their peak and just as devoted to staying at the state-of-the-art as their peers in other professions. Search Amazon.com, however, and you'll discover that there's not a single book devoted to the principles and practices of effective career self-management for recruiters. And yet, they have endured just as many or more layoffs and been affected by just as many restructuring initiatives as any other function in the enterprise.

How can you protect yourself and your recruiting career in such a demanding environment?

IMPLEMENT THE FOLLOWING NEXT PRACTICES:
Don't Believe in Fairy Tales
Renewable Recruiting Excellence
The Right to Be Remembered
Get the Career You Deserve
The Mindful Recruiter

Don't Believe in Fairy Tales

For decades, economists celebrated the rational person. It was their view that people would always make the intelligent choice – do what was in their best interests – when making a decision that would affect their economic wellbeing. Then, in the 1970s, two psychologists debunked that idea and one went on the win the Nobel Prize, in economics no less, for doing so. Turns out, we humans aren't as clear headed as we think we are, and that truism offers an important message for recruiters.

Daniel Kahneman and his collaborator Amos Tversky conducted a series of experiments that proved we humans do not always live our lives to "maximize utility." Instead, the rational side of our brain, which is lazy and tends to tire quickly, often defers to the emotional side, which is quick to act and doesn't let facts get in the way. Kahneman describes these different approaches as "thinking, fast and slow," which just happens to also be the name of a book he's written.

Why is this distinction important to recruiters? Because, all too often, we let the emotional side of our brain guide us in the management of our own careers.

Our rational mind will collect facts, analyze their importance to and potential impact on us, and then determine a course of action which will maximize their benefit for us. In the case of recruiters, these facts include the following:

> While the economy is recovering, it is still vulnerable to being thrown back into a recession or worse by a cascade of events or even a single crisis in one or more of the world's developing nations, the European Union or such hot spots as the Middle East.

> Thanks to intense competition in the global marketplace, employers are now quick to act whenever the economy slows, and the first step they take is to cut labor costs, and among the first categories of labor to see their jobs disappear are recruiters.

These facts are real and have the potential to harm or even derail our career. Yet, as Kahneman notes, many of us ignore them. We let the emotional side of our brain take over, and it is guided by what he calls "a pervasive optimistic bias" – a hard-wired positive outlook that colors our perceptions of both the world around us and its prospects for our own lives.

Despite the facts, we assume (a) our employer will always be a healthy enterprise, (b) our supervisor will always make intelligent and unbiased decisions, and (c) our job will always be there for us. We are smart enough to know otherwise, of course, but all too often we choose to believe the fairy tale.

Making the Rational Choice

In a workplace governed by uncertainty and the looming threat of unemployment, no rational person would ignore taking steps to protect themselves from such eventualities. Yet, many of us in recruiting, focus so exclusively on doing our jobs, we ignore our careers. We devote 8, 9, 10 hours a day, 5, 6 and sometimes even 7 days a week to maximizing the benefits for our employers and thus have no time or energy left to do what might benefit us.

I would respectfully suggest that such behavior is irresponsible or as Kahneman would describe it, irrational. It exposes our job, our career and our family to unnecessary risk and potentially grave harm.

What should we be doing?

Delivering the best work we can for our employer – building job security – and putting equal priority on the work we do for our own economic wellbeing – building "career security." Or to put it in business terms, we should be loyal to our employers and to ourselves. We should be looking for talent <u>and</u> for what might be our next job.

Because here's another fact our rational mind should assess:

Even when business is slowing and the stock market is falling, there are always segments of the economy that are thriving, so even when the news is filled with gloom and doom, four-fifths of the population is able to find work.

In today's uncertain and hyper dynamic world, making rational decisions about a career is not only prudent, it's absolutely essential to success. We can be as optimistic as we like, but that optimism should always be tempered with a respect for the facts.

Renewable Recruiting Excellence

Sourcing and recruiting are hard work. At least, if they're done right, they are. And hard work performed without let-up or recuperation time has serious repercussions. It wears you out, saps your productivity and drains your creativity. In short, unrelenting hard work sets you up for failure.

As anybody with more than fifteen minutes of experience knows, there is too much work for too few hands in today's workplace. Whether it's called "doing more with less" or "a strategy to improve productivity," the end result is the same. Every recruiter is drowning in a tsunami of unending requirements, deadlines and pressure.

This environment is a threat to recruiters' well being and their careers. They enjoy their work, so they should come home exhausted but fulfilled by their accomplishments. Today, however, exactly the opposite is happening. More and more recruiters feel exhausted before they even get to work. They are depleted of energy and thus unable to perform at their peak.

Consider some of the data presented in a recent article in *The New York Times*, entitled "Relax! You'll be More Productive."

> More than one-third of employees now eat their lunch at their desks so they can keep plowing through the unfinished work piled there.

> More than half of all workers assume they will be one of those people lying on the beach somewhere and checking office email while they are "on vacation."

> A growing number of people don't even bother to pretend they're on vacation – on average, Americans didn't use over nine of the vacation days they had earned in 2012.

This situation is simply unsustainable, at least if the goal is to have sourcers and recruiters do their best work on-the-job. Which begs the question: how do you establish a strategy for renewable recruiting excellence?

What the Research Shows

According to that article in the *Times*, we humans need to be reinvigorated in at least two different ways. One, of course, is periodic breaks that last more than a day or two. Those breaks are called "vacations," but they live up to that name only if one is able to vacate the premises, both literally <u>and</u> virtually.

No less important, however, is the surprising conclusion by a growing body of multidisciplinary research. It discovered that we humans have a finite capacity for excellence that is measured in much shorter increments. We need to pause and stop what we're doing every 90 minutes or so if we want to deliver peak productivity and performance on-the-job.

These breaks need not be lengthy – 20-30 minutes is sufficient – must they must be filled with recuperative activity. For example, if a person breaks to fight with their spouse or talk to a teacher about a problem their child is having at school, they might as well keep working. The stress or anxiety of the pause will wear them down just as much as a meeting with an obtuse hiring manager.

What kinds of activities provide genuine recuperation? Naps, of course, can do the trick, which is why more and more employers are actually setting aside special rooms for employees to catch a couple of winks. And, at the other end of the spectrum, a physical interlude – a walk or brief work-out – can also clear the mind and help recharge a person's batteries.

While employers should take the lead on introducing renewable recruiting excellence – after all, they're the ones that benefit from the higher levels of productivity and performance it produces - sourcers and recruiters will probably have to get it done on their own. Thankfully, there's plenty of research with which to make the case, but why go to all that trouble? What's in it for them?

The ultimate beneficiaries of renewable recruiting excellence are sourcers and recruiters themselves. Their health improves. Their enthusiasm is replenished. And their capacity to do their best work is restored. In today's economy, those attributes pay a double dividend: they increase both the respect and the satisfaction a person brings home from work.

The Right to Be Remembered

Privacy advocates are fighting for the right to be forgotten on the Web. Online mistakes are visible to everyone, so we need to be sure they won't live on forever. In today's workplace, however, we require a different kind of guarantee. We need to preserve our right to be remembered.

It used to be that managing your career was a lot like riding a bicycle. With an occasional pump of the peddles, you could coast for quite awhile and still move forward. Rely on such a leisurely pace today, and you're likely to suffer a violent crash or what most of us call unemployment.

Why?

Because many our employers are now suffering from "employment dementia." They don't recognize all of the contributions we've made to their success in the past, and they can't remember what we did for them just the other day. Our track records have faded away, and our contributions have been lost.

This condition isn't something employers chose to experience. It's been imposed on them by the fierce competition they face in the global marketplace. That challenge comes at them without let up and from every direction. The pressure is intense, the demands are enormous. In such an environment, survival (let alone success) demands ever higher levels of performance from everyone on the payroll. The only thing employers remember is "what you can do for them next" rather than "what you did for them in the past."

Reinforcing Your Employer's Memory

Being remembered begins with being proactive in your career's management. As I describe in *The Career Fitness Workbook*, building a healthy career is just like building up your physical fitness. You have to take personal responsibility for making it happen, and you have to work on it every single day.

And that's a challenge. We humans are prone to a fitness-sapping disease called *OBE – overtaken by events*. We do all the right things – we set goals for our career, we start exercising to increase its strength, reach and endurance – and then life gets in the way. Our boss or our job suddenly needs our full attention, and our self-improvement get sacrificed.

How can you avoid this debilitating situation? Do all the right things <u>and</u> monitor your progress. Give yourself a Quarterly Performance Review. Sit down quietly and evaluate your progress. If you've stuck to your career exercising regimen, give yourself a pat on the back; it you've let your commitment slip, determine how best to get back on track.

Finally, ask yourself if you're making sufficient progress to be remembered. How can you tell? The effort you've made in the previous quarter must have produced a "career victory" – an advance in your knowledge, skills, ability, wisdom, or experience that's worth telling others about. In other words, the outcome of each 90-day commitment to building career fitness should be a memory – a memory that you share with your boss and your employer.

That's the secret to achieving durable employment security in a demanding global marketplace. You do it by being remembered over and over again.

Get the Career You Deserve

After the last recession, recruiters have to be asking themselves, "How do I have a meaningful career in this field of work?". The minute the economy goes south, the nanosecond hiring slows, recruiters get their pink slips. There is no job security in recruiting. You can however, create something even better: *career security*.

Career security is the ability always to be employed and always by an employer of your choice. If you think that's a pipe dream, consider this: between February and April of 2010, more Americans resigned from their jobs (2.0 million) than were laid off (1.7 million). A cohort of the American workforce as large as the city of Houston decided they could work wherever it best suited them, not the other way around. That's career security in action.

Contrast it with the faux promise of job security. In survey after survey, job security is the #1 goal of working Americans. Yet, it is something they can't control – employers do – and it's something that only works when times are good – when they don't need it.

> How do you achieve career security? By taking charge of the direction and shape of your career.

Recruiters are the only profession in which its members spend all day, every day, promoting the careers of others. If recruiting were a religion, they'd all be candidates for sainthood. But, as anyone who's been in the field for more than five minutes knows, recruiting is a profession. And, professional people are only as successful as they are competent in managing their own careers. In other words, the sole way to achieve career security is to be proficient and proactive in *career self-management.*

Become an Expert in Career Self-Management

The challenge for many recruiters today is that virtually all of the training they take, all of the conference presentations they attend, and all of the recruitment-related publications they read focus on just one aspect of what it takes to be a successful recruiting professional. They are inundated with content designed to expand their expertise in sourcing and recruiting, but told nothing at all about what else they must do to achieve career security.

What are those other activities? They are the seven essential steps of what I call **Career Fitness** – a system of principles and practices for proactively building a career that will steadily increase both the paycheck and the satisfaction you bring home from your work.

To build Career Fitness, you must devote the time and make the effort to attend to ALL of the following:

Pump up your Career Cardiovascular System.
The heart of your career is the range and depth of your expertise in recruiting. It has to be at the state-of-the-art, but unlike what many pundits now suggest, that includes both the latest techniques and those that are well established but still effective.

Strengthen Your Career Circulatory System.
The circulatory system of your career is your network of professional contacts and connections. The wider and deeper that network, the more visible you and your capabilities will be in the workplace.

Develop All of Your Career Muscle Groups.
The muscle groups of your career are the ancillary skills and knowledge you bring to work (e.g., a second language, the ability to lead a team). The broader your set of capabilities, the wider the range of situations and assignments in which you can be employed.

Increase Your Career Flexibility & Range of Motion.
The flexibility and range of motion in your career dictate your willingness and ability to adapt to new circumstances and requirements. The greater those attributes, the more proactive you can be in directing your career.

Work With Winners.
The environment in which you work can either enable and empower you or frustrate and even derail you. Working for the right employer with the right coworkers is the only way to ensure you have an unfettered shot at being the best you can be.

Pace Yourself.
The pace you set for your career dictates your resilience and endurance on-the-job and the creativity, innovation and imagination you bring to your work. The right pace ensures that you can perform at your peak even in times of high demand and over the long arc of your entire career.

Stretch Your Soul.
Your talent – your capacity for excellence in your chosen field of work – is a gift. When you contribute that talent in service to others – a social service or civic organization, for example – you promote their well being and nurture your soul.

Taking an active role in building your Career Fitness as a recruiting professional is not something you should do. It's something you (and your career) deserve. It enables you to be the best you can be and, as a result, to experience the financial and spiritual benefits of career security.

The Mindful Recruiter

Recruiters fill one of the most stressful and least appreciated jobs in the workplace. They are bombarded with requirements, complaints, constraints and administrivia, and they get precious little support, recognition or gratitude in return. How can we do their best work in such a hostile environment? With mindfulness.

Mindfulness has suddenly caught the attention of working Americans. It's as if we've reached a tipping point in our hyper-paced and ultra-demanding careers and have collectively begun to search for ways to find some calm and quiet in our work. We know we can't turn off the spigot of day-to-day requisitions, job postings, social media connections, interviews, hiring manager conferences and offer letters, but we also know we have to find a balance to it all or we're likely to burn out.

Wikipedia defines mindfulness as "the focusing of attention and awareness, based on the concept of mindfulness in Buddhist meditation." It's now practiced in many places, however, without a religious context. It can sound a little "new agey" at first, but its principles are both physiologically and psychologically sound.

I call mindfulness in recruiting a way to "pay attention to ourselves." It is an alternative approach to working in the pressure-packed, adrenalin soaked culture of today's "doing more with less" workplace. Mindfulness is not a prescription for ignoring our job, but instead a permission slip to care for ourselves, so we can do a better job.

Mindfulness provides a set of practices for reducing job-induced pressure and stress. It is a schedule of breaks built, not around the water cooler or Facebook, but around the soothing effects of body rhythms and peacefulness. Yes, it's meditation, but it's meditation with an occupational purpose – to counter the injurious effects of roadblocks we face in the present and to fend off the effects of other roadblocks we are likely to confront in the future.

Paying Attention to Yourself

Recruiters face a daily obstacle course of insensitive or inept hiring managers, unrealistic or back-breaking requisitions and mind-numbing or convoluted administrative requirements. It can sap our self-confidence, commitment to excellence and even our ability to care about our job.

Working harder doesn't redress those symptoms. Only paying attention to ourselves can do that. How? By interspersing our work with periods of self-rejuvenation. Research has shown that adults need a break every ninety minutes or so, if they are to keep themselves stimulated and performing at their peak. And, they also need such breaks to repair themselves after the particularly stressful events that can occur from time-to-time in any career.

The mindful recruiter uses these breaks for meditation. They focus on their breathing – on listening to the rhythm of their body. If their respiration is at its natural pace, they concentrate on simply experiencing that gift of life. And, if it's ragged or rapid from the stress of the day, they slowly and steadily move it back to its natural state.

In both cases, they inhale to reinforce their spirit and sense of purpose in their work and exhale to eradicate the toxins of stress and anxiety that the workplace has produced. With each breath in, they say quietly to themselves *I remember who I am*, and with each breathe out, they say *I rejoice in who I am*.

So, if you're stressed from the workload of a seemingly interminable list of requisitions, take a periodic break to pay attention to you. And, if you feel like you've been tossed in a pressure cooker after a meeting with some hiring manager, take a break then, as well, and take care of yourself.

Stress, anxiety, pressure – they all cloud our ability to recognize or remember our inherent value as a person and our contribution at work. Mindfulness is a way for recruiters to recapture both in the daily rhythms of their life.

About the Author

Peter Weddle has been the CEO of three HR consulting companies, a Partner in the Hay Group and the recipient of a Federal award for leadership-related research. Described by *The Washington Post* as "... a man filled with ingenious ideas," he has authored or edited over two dozen books and been a columnist for *The Wall Street Journal, National Business Employment Weekly* and CNN.com.

Weddle is the Executive Director of the International Association of Employment Web Sites (www.EmploymentWebSites. org), the trade association for the global online employment services industry, and the CEO of WEDDLE's Research & Publications which specializes in employment and workforce issues. The American Staffing Association has described *WEDDLE's Guide to Employment Sites* on the Internet as the "Zagat of the online employment industry."

Weddle is a graduate of the United States Military Academy at West Point. He attended Oxford University and holds advanced degrees from Middlebury College and Harvard University.

WEDDLE's Books for Corporate Recruiting Teams

Available at Amazon.com or Weddles.com

WEDDLE's Guide to Employment Sites on the Internet
Called the Zagat of the online employment services industry, this guide includes WEDDLE's choice for The Top 100, the best job boards and social media sites on the Web, and The Best & the Rest, a directory of over 9,000 sites organized by career field, industry and other factors.

WEDDLE's Guide to Association Web Sites
This one-of-a-kind guide provides a listing of the online employment resources available at over 3,000 professional societies and trade associations.

WEDDLE's Directory of Employment Sites on the Internet
This one-of-a-kind database of job boards, social media sites, career portals, aggregators, employment-related search engines, job ad distribution companies, recruitment blogs and other recruiter resources includes 9,000+ entries organized by occupational field, industry and geographic focus. The database is delivered to users online and is both internally searchable and suitable for downloading into a CRM system.

The Sourcing & Recruiting Handbook
Source better, smarter, faster, and cheaper than the competition
By Shally Steckerl
The Sourcing & Recruiting Handbook is the most extensive and up-to-date resource for Internet sourcing and recruiting, period. It is a one-of-a-kind guide to Shally Steckerl's trade secrets for finding talent online. With over 450 pages covering all the latest trends, tools, tips and tricks of the trade, it will help you source better, smarter, faster, and cheaper than the competition.

Finding Needles in a Haystack
Keywords for Finding Top Talent
By Wendy Enelow
Whether you're searching for top prospects on LinkedIn or Facebook, in the resume databases on job boards or in your own ATS, this three-book set is the perfect resource for you. *Finding Needles in a Haystack* provides over 25,000 keywords and keyword phrases, across 5,400 job and position titles in 28 industries and professions. You can order each book separately or the 3-volume set.

Volume I: Engineering, Executive & Management, Finance & Economics, Healthcare, Human Resources, Sales & Marketing, Technology

Volume II: Banking, Broadcasting & Media, Construction, Dentistry, Food & Beverage, Hospitality, Insurance, Investment Finance, Law, Pharmacy, Psychology & Counseling, Real Estate, Retail, Science, Social Work & Services

Volume III: Accounting & Bookkeeping, Administration, Advertising & Communications, Architecture, Art & Design, Customer Service, Equipment Installation & Maintenance,

Hazardous Materials, Manufacturing, Public Relations, Purchasing, Security, Translation, Logistics, Writing

The Career Fitness Workbook
How to Find, Win & Hang Onto the Job of Your Dreams
By Peter Weddle

This self-paced instructional guide introduces a complete regimen of seven career-building activities that will help you successfully compete for and excel at the job of your dreams. Its step-by-step, detailed guidelines will strengthen your prospects for success, whether you're in transition or looking to advance in your field. It's a winning resource for everyone from recent graduates to seasoned professionals and even senior executives.

The Career Activist Republic
By Peter Weddle

This blockbuster of a book provides a provocative yet positive assessment of the changing world of work in the American economy and describes an innovative strategy that will enable you to avoid the pitfalls and capture the opportunities in this new environment.

Generalship: *HR Leadership in a Time of War*
By Peter Weddle

There are plenty of books on HR management, but this hardback is the only primer on leadership written expressly for HR professionals. Using lessons drawn from great generals in the past, it offers innovative insights for winning the War for Relevancy in the modern enterprise and the War for Talent in the 21st Century.

The A+ Solution: *How America's Professional Societies and Trade Associations Can Solve the Nation's Workforce Skills Crisis*
By John Bell & Christine Smith

Too many of America's workers lack the skills and knowledge to work in a highly competitive global economy. To date, the Federal Government has largely relied on promoting access to academic institutions to solve this problem. *The A+ Solution*, in contrast, offers both a convincing rationale and a detailed strategy for tapping the education and training resources of America's professional societies and trade associations.